Yellow Umbrella Books are published by Red Brick Learning
7825 Telegraph Road, Bloomington, Minnesota 55438
http://www.redbricklearning.com

Library of Congress Cataloging-in-Publication Data
Ring, Susan.
     [I see patterns. Spanish & English]
     I see patterns/by Susan Ring = Veo patrónes/por Susan Ring.
     p. cm.
     Summary: "Simple text and photos present some of the patterns in nature and in
everyday things"—Provided by publisher.
     Includes index.
     ISBN-13: 978-0-7368-6014-7 (hardcover)
     ISBN-10: 0-7368-6014-2 (hardcover)
     1. Pattern perception—Juvenile literature. 2. Pattern formation (Physical sciences)—
Juvenile literature. I. Title: Veo patrónes. II. Title.
Q327.R5618 2006
152.14'23—dc22   2005025845

Written by Susan Ring
Developed by Raindrop Publishing

Editorial Director: Mary Lindeen
Editor: Jennifer VanVoorst
Photo Researcher: Wanda Winch
Adapted Translations: Gloria Ramos
Spanish Language Consultants: Jesús Cervantes, Anita Constantino
Conversion Assistants: Jenny Marks, Laura Manthe

Photo Credits
Cover: Digital Vision; Title Page: Digital Stock; Page 4: Ralf Schmode; Page 6: Keith
Wood/Corbis; Page 8: Paul Hartley/Image Ideas, Inc.; Page 10: David Frazier/Corbis; Page
12: Heinz Hubler/RubberBall; Page 14: Gary Sundermeyer/Capstone Press; Page 16: Paul
Hartley/Image Ideas, Inc.

1 2 3 4 5 6 11 10 09 08 07 06

I See Patterns

by Susan Ring

Veo patrones

por Susan Ring

Yellow Umbrella Books
for early readers

I see patterns on the tiger.

Veo patrones en el tigre.

I see patterns in the sand.

Veo patrones en la arena.

I see patterns on
the butterfly.

Veo patrones en
la mariposa.

I see patterns on the land.

Veo patrones en la tierra.

I see patterns on
the flags.

Veo patrones en
las banderas.

I see patterns by the sea.

Veo patrones en la playa.

I even see patterns
on a bee!

También veo patrones
en la abeja.

Index

Índice